MW00559618

ARRANGED AND PERFORMED BY TONY MIZEN

HAL•LEONARD® CORPORATION

7777 W. BLUEMOUND RD. P.O. BOX 13819 MILWAUKEE, WI 53213

Publisher: Jim Beloff
Edited by Ronny S. Schiff
Cover and Art Direction by Elizabeth Maihock Beloff
Graphics and Music Typography by Georgina Combe and Charylu Roberts
Cover Ukulele Photo by Rick Scanlan

Visit us on the web at **www.fleamarketmusic.com**

Biography

Tony Mizen began playing the guitar at the age of fourteen. After several years of strumming chords, he was hooked first by flamenco guitar and then classical guitar, with inspiration from several excellent teachers. He came in First Place four years in a row at a guitar festival in Kent, and after passing his performer's diploma, he started teaching the guitar full time in various schools.

Several years ago, Tony was asked if he could teach the ukulele. He knew nothing about the instrument but agreed to the task, swiftly buying a ukulele and instruction book! Since that day, the ukulele has been an absorbing interest for Tony. He was delighted to discover the Victoria College of Music in London, UK, which takes the instrument seriously enough to produce an entire exam syllabus. Tony took the Performer's Diploma in 2010, passing with Distinction. He is the first and currently, only person in the UK to have a diploma in the ukulele. His first book/CD, *From Lute to Uke*, was published by Flea Market Music in 2011.

Credits

Many thanks to Jim Beloff for inviting me to do another book and CD, as well as sending me the beautiful Fluke that I used for the recording. Thank you to Georgina Combe who engraved the music from my handwritten scrawl and to Charylu Roberts and Ronny Schiff for the many hours they spent on the editing and preparation.

Thank you to Dale Nash for doing the recording and mastering at Audio Sorcery Studios, Wadhurst, near Tunbridge Wells, Kent, UK; and to Robert Bedwell for reading my draft on the history of Baroque music. His awesome knowledge and expertise on music gives me the confidence that this part is free from error!

Thanks to St.John Asprey for the photograph.

A special thank you to the uke enthusiasts on various Internet forums who have written many encouraging words about my first ukulele book, *From Lute to Uke*, and who asked for another volume. Here it is! I hope you enjoy playing these pieces and feel it adds to the repertoire of this lovely instrument.

Mizen

The Evolution Of Baroque Music

In *From Lute to Uke,* I found it helpful to compare the development of the lute to a natural evolutionary process. The lute was seen to have "evolved" from the Arabian oud, migrating and adapting to different environments until a new, distinct species emerged. This analogy continues to be useful when looking at how music itself has changed over the centuries.

Western music is generally divided up into the following "species": Medieval (before 1450), Renaissance (1450-1600), Baroque (1600-1750), Classical (1750-1830), Romantic (early and late; 1830-1860 / 1860-1920) and Modern (1920 to present). Each of these species has adapted to its own specific time, place and culture and it is tempting to compare them with natural species that still exist today: the fish, amphibians, reptiles, birds and mammals. All these species—both animal and musical—have a common ancestor, have undergone changes from what was already there, and have adapted to new environments. Thanks to their robust nature and a little bit of conservation, they have survived.

Renaissance music of Europe evolved from Medieval music. Melodies and dances that developed among the population were altered and "purified" by the church, subjecting them to its own rules. Words during church services became beautified when recited as chants, but the instinct for secular song and dance did not abate.

Renaissance music flourished for several hundred years with more complex rhythms and more dissonances to create a feeling of tension and movement. Music at this time was based on a simple system of "modes." Essentially, this is a single musical scale where any note in that scale can be used as the starting note.

The modern scale of C major is also known as the Ionian mode. The notes C D E F G A B C give us that familiar sound that everyone knows! But if you play from the second note: D E F G A B C D, the sound and feel is different. You have played the same notes in a different order, but your brain just doesn't recognize it as the same, because the pattern of intervals between the notes has now shifted. This is the Dorian mode and it has that distinctive "folksy" and Renaissance feel. You could continue to play the same scale from the third, fourth, fifth, sixth and seventh notes. Each mode has a different name, sound, mood and even culture.

Modal music did not die out. It still occurs in folk music around the world, some rock music, flamenco, classical and jazz. But during the Baroque period, a new system and set of rules came into being. Instead of using one scale of notes, all notes, it was discovered, could be used to create different "keys." If we take the C major scale again: C D E F G A B C, every note of this scale can be used to create the same pattern of intervals by using sharps and flats. We can create a G major scale by starting on G and sharpening the F, for example. We can create a D major scale by sharpening the F and the C and so on. We now have so much more material with which to play. Baroque composers could then write more complex music that changed key (modulated) and much of the skill was discovering how to do this in a satisfying way. There was just one problem…

Early keyboard instruments like the clavichord and virginals were fine for playing in the modal system, but when changing to a completely different key, they sounded out of tune. Bach's compositions for the *Well Tempered Clavier* demonstrate a resolution to this problem. The idea of "equal temperament" is to make a compromise with all the possible keys until all notes sound correct, no matter in what key you are playing (it's a matter of physics). This goes some way to explain one of the most confusing aspects of music—why there appears to be two names for the same notes, for example B flat and A sharp. In acoustic reality, these two notes are slightly different but have been made to function as one. These "enharmonics" are referred to by different names depending upon the key of the music.

Bach's "Prelude in C major" is a perfect example of a well-tempered keyboard piece. This beautiful piece moves effortlessly through many different keys without producing that shocked feeling we might experience in modern pop music when there is an abrupt change of key, usually towards the end of the song. Bach's *Twenty-four Preludes and Fugues* are played in all possible keys and demonstrate the success of equal temperament.

With the continued use and importance of the harpsichord tuned to equal temperament, other instruments of the time were forced to comply, firmly establishing the tonal system as the official and civilized way of making music. Eventually, the success of the modern piano would threaten to drive the harpsichord to extinction.

The Baroque period witnessed the rise of other stronger, louder instruments such as the 'cello and the modern violin. This enabled more expressive music to be written incorporating new techniques. Ornamentation became more elaborate with the use of trills and mordents and other forms of decoration. Musicians had different ideas in different regions of Europe, but nowhere did ornamentation become more intense than in France. The new styles and elaborate techniques led to the description of this music as "Baroque," which alludes to an "oddly shaped" pearl as opposed to the smooth pearl of the Renaissance.

What survived from the Renaissance became more elaborate. Baroque composers such as J.S. Bach and Handel continued to create suites of dances, usually comprised of the following: Allemande, Courante, Sarabande, Gigue, Gavotte and Minuet. The great skill of these composers was to put the same melodic idea through the various dance forms, creating variety and interest. Doubtless, this could be done through on the spot improvisation, much like a jazz musician.

Bach's death marks the end of the Baroque era and the beginning of a new style characterized by the emphasis on symmetry and "perfection" in music as seen in the music of Mozart and Haydn of the Classical era.

Arranging For The Ukulele

In *From Lute to Uke*, the task of arranging the pieces for ukulele was fairly straightforward. In most of the examples, wherever possible and practical, I read the melody from guitar transcriptions. Due to the different tunings of the two instruments, this meant that the notes of the melody were four notes higher than written. Here is a comparison between the four open strings of the ukulele and the first four open strings of the guitar, starting with the fourth string showing the four-note difference between them:

Guitar: D G B E vs. Ukulele: G C E A

Harmony notes therefore had to be raised by four notes to match the melody. Any note below middle C had to be raised an octave or omitted.

In *The Baroque Ukulele*, I did essentially the same thing but this time I worked from piano music in some pieces. Plus, there was one piano and flute duet, and a concerto consisting of a guitar part, two violins, a viola and a 'cello. Knowing the bass clef and C clef was useful here, although I ended up leaving out anything played by the viola in the concerto. The bass parts tended to be quite simple and formed my notes on the third string of the ukulele. The violins I and II were the same throughout, so the arranging for the concerto became easier than it first looked.

About The Arrangements

Chorale: This is one of many compositions that found its way into two manuscript books that J.S. Bach created for his second wife, Anna Magdalena. For over twenty years, the books expanded with entries from friends and Bach's children, becoming something of a family album. An accomplished clavier player herself, Anna must have loved playing these pieces. There are no real technical or rhythmic difficulties for the ukulele player with this piece. Even a complete beginner could play it after just a short time.

Menuet en Rondeau: This short and pleasant tune was written for the harpsichord, the instrument most associated with Rameau. In the 1980s, the band SKY included Rameau's "Gavotte avec 6 Doubles" on their album *SKY 2*. This wonderfully stirring music was my first introduction to Rameau, which led me to his harpsichord suites with their intricate ornamentations and flourishes so characteristic of French Baroque music. This simple tune has no difficulties though and with some imagination, the harpsichord sound is still present in the music.

Winter from *The Four Seasons*: A tune well known to many all over the world. Vivaldi wrote over five hundred pieces but *The Four Seasons* is what always stands out. In this tune, the first of several ornaments is introduced. For help in executing the trill, please see "The Symbols Used In The Music" section.

Spring from *The Four Seasons*: Only two of the four seasons seemed viable for the ukulele. This short extract is a bright cheering melody, conjuring up the sound of bird song. The musical style is unmistakable and has even made a comeback in modern times in so-called neo-Baroque music. The modern composer Karl Jenkins, for example, pays a tribute to Vivaldi with his terrific *Palladio*.

Playing this tune on the ukulele is made easier with the use of *barrés* as indicated. Also, when there is a G standing on its own, as in measures 13 and 20, there is always a choice between the open fourth string or fret three on string two. Choose whichever feels easier.

Bourrée from J.S. Bach's *Fourth Cello Suite*: This dance movement works perfectly on the ukulele. Once mastered, counting four quarter notes a bar, try shifting to a feeling of two half notes a bar. This is what your foot should tap naturally with this dance form.

The Harmonious Blacksmith: This is the well-known theme from the final movement of Handel's *Air and Variations Suite no. 5 in E Major* for harpsichord. There are various claims for the title, but the most likely appears to be a blacksmith turned-music-seller named William Lintern. He called himself "the harmonious blacksmith" and printed the Handel movement as a separate piece under that title. Before the days of copyright, the Italian guitarist Mauro Giuliani used the tune to write his own set of variations.

Rondeau from *Symphonies de Fanfares*: A *rondo* (or the French *rondeau*) is a musical form where there is a return of a principal theme between several other musical "episodes." The ear latches onto what it has heard before and anticipates its return. Like life itself, in music we need a mixture of variety and familiarity for enjoyment and appreciation. In one way or another, all musical forms achieve this. Despite a successful musical career, it appears that the later years of composer Jean-Joseph Mouret's life were beset with financial and psychological problems. It is said that his jealousy of Rameau drove him to madness. Would he have been happier if he knew that the "Rondeau" was adapted as the theme of the PBS program *Masterpiece Theatre* and now is a musical choice for many weddings?

Musette: The following two pieces are found in the *Anna Magdalena Bach Notebook* mentioned in the notes for the *Chorale*. They are both generally attributed to J.S. Bach, but officially they are contributions from anonymous/unknown composers. A *musette* is a kind of French bagpipe and here the music may be imitating the instrument with repeated drone notes. In the first half up to the repeat, anchoring finger two on "G" at fret three, string two, provides a base for the other fingers to move securely.

Menuet: A very well known tune, and like the *Musette*, taken directly from the *Anna Magdalena Bach Notebook* piano score. Many of the notes had to be edited out, however the essential melody and harmony work perfectly on the ukulele, and quite easy to play as well.

Pièce Pour Luth: Although written during the middle Baroque period, this piece sounds decidedly Renaissance and modal—a style that this Polish composer, Bartlomiej Pekiel was at home with. He wrote over 40 instrumental pieces, 14 masses and 12 motets, and yet he and his music are far from well known. However, several CDs of his music have been recorded.

Gavotto: I have selected three of my favorite dances by guitar, lute and theorbo composer, Robert de Visée. Well known to guitarists, the composer wrote two books of guitar music consisting of twelve suites. However, these three also work perfectly well on the ukulele.

Minuet II: It is easy to visualize this tune as a dance, with its characteristic small steps. There are no real difficulties in playing this piece, as long as you can hold down a barré at the fifth fret. This occurs three times. In measure 17, the little finger is used to play the lowest note of the third beat (F sharp). If this proves to be too difficult, it can be left out without spoiling the music.

Sarabande from *Suite in D Minor*: The *sarabande* is a Spanish dance where the accent falls mainly on the second beat of the measure. There is a haunting, profundity to this dance. This example is particularly beautiful transposed to G minor from the original D minor. It also has both upper and lower mordents to decorate the melody. An explanation of how to execute these is found in "The Symbols Used In The Music" section.

Gavotte from *Sonata No. 9 in B Flat*: Corelli is a very important figure in the age of baroque music. He was considered to be one of the greatest violinists of his time and greatly sought out as a teacher in Rome where he spent most of his life. This piece works well on the ukulele and makes a good imitation of the violin.

Largo from *Xerxes*: Although not explicitly melancholy, this piece from a Handel opera is played often at funerals. The music exudes emotion and has a certain "truth" about it that goes deep. I made it playable by changing the octaves in several places. The small circle in bar 15 indicates a "harmonic," wherein you lightly touch the first string at the twelfth fret as you pluck the string at the same time. With practice, you should get a bell-like sound that sings out.

Air on a G String from the *Orchestral Suite No. 3 in D Major*: Another wonderful and well-known Bach piece from the suite's second movement. The title apparently comes from an arrangement of the music made by August Wilhelmj for violin and piano. By transposing the key from D major to C major, the melody could be played entirely on the violin's G string.

Sleepers Wake: The title for this chorale cantata by J.S. Bach originates from a text by Philip Nicolai (1599) based on the *Parable of the Ten Virgins* (Matthew 25:1-3). The first line translates to "Wake up, the voice is calling us." There are one or two difficult bars in this arrangement and I have put in some suggested left-hand fingerings to help.

Canon: Pachelbel's famous "Canon in D Major" has become "Canon in C Major" in this arrangement. After trying out many different examples, I eventually found one for flute and piano that seemed to work for the ukulele with some manipulation! Originally, the music was written for three violins and basso continuo. The violins play the same musical phrases at different entry points as defines a round or a canon. After being forgotten for many years, it was re-discovered in 1919 and has been very popular and greatly loved since.

The Prince of Denmark's March: This is the first of two well-known tunes for trumpet arranged for ukulele. This piece by Jeremiah Clarke is also known as "Trumpet Voluntary." A convincing execution of the trill is clearly the difficulty here. Where the trill is indicated in the first measure, it is best to use fingers 1 and 2 for the B and G sharp. This made finger 3 available for the upper note of the trill, instead of using finger 4, which tends to be less obedient to your brain's commands. Once under control, exactly the same trill is needed another five times. The trills in measures 9 and 13 are only possible using a barré.

Trumpet Tune: I have kept with convention and music books here and attributed this famous piece to Henry Purcell, however it has been suggested that Jeremiah Clarke composed this piece instead. There are fewer trills in this second trumpet tune, but it still has its challenges. Measure 23 needs careful playing with finger 4 taking the eleventh fret on the third string.

Bourrée: Silvius Leopold Weiss was a great composer for the Baroque lute and lived at the same time as J.S. Bach. They knew each other and engaged in friendly competitions as to who could improvise the best. There is something particularly distinctive, melodic and accessible to Weiss' music, as I hope this piece demonstrates. Here is another example where ornamentation is used. I have provided an alternative ending for those who have only twelve frets on their ukuleles.

Concerto for Lute, 2 Violins and Basso continuo in D Major RV93:

Movement I – Allegro guisto: After *The Four Seasons*, Vivaldi's numerous concerti are still much loved and much performed. I worked with two versions of this concerto, taking measures from both to make it as easy as possible and moving the piece to G major. Despite this, the arrangement remains a challenge for the ukulele player. Playing the music for several instruments reduced to four strings was never going to be easy! Keep the triplets nice and steady from measures 29 to 34.

Movement II – Largo: In contrast to the first movement, this beautiful, peaceful melody is very easy to play apart from the first couple of notes in measure 21. This takes a few goes to get right, but the smooth *campanella* result is worth the effort.

Movement III – Allegro: This final movement took a lot of adjustment, again selecting from two different versions. To imitate the sound of all instruments playing together in measures 15 to 17, I strum the chords up and down with my index finger. Some left-hand fingerings and positions have been added to help with the challenges from measures 29 onwards.

The Symbols Used In The Music

In these arrangements, the following ornaments are used. These are all examples of how melody was decorated in Baroque music:

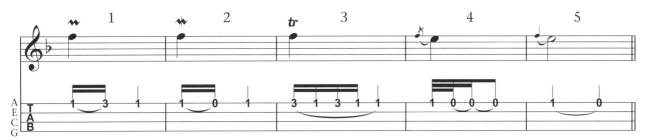

1. **Mordent:** Decoration of the quarter note by slurring up a note and back to the main note.

2. **Inverted mordent:** Decoration of a quarter note by slurring down to the note below and then back to the main note.

3. **Trill:** In the Baroque era, the trill sign above a chord means that you play the trill on the highest note in the chord. It is therefore important to refer to the TAB when executing these ornaments. In the notation, the highest note in the chord is not always the note that requires the trill.

4. **Acciaccatura:** A "crushed in" note played as rapidly as possible in front of the main note.

5. **Appoggiatura:** A note that "leans" on the main note. The appoggiatura generally takes half the value of the note that follows it.

10/2015

TRACK 1

Chorale
From *The Anna Magdalena Bach Notebooks*

Johann Sebastian Bach
(1685-1750)

Ukulele

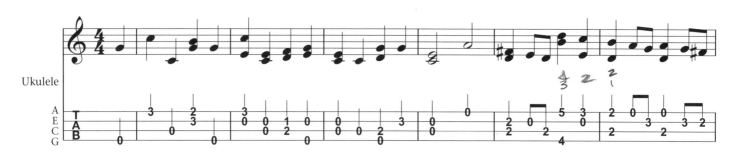

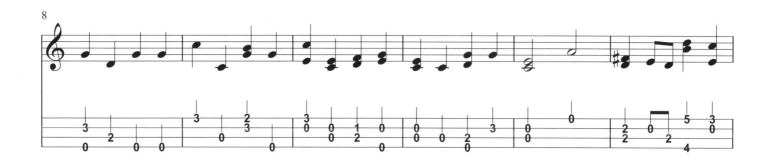

TRACK 2

Menuet en Rondeau

Jean-Philippe Rameau
(1683 -1764)

Ukulele

Winter
From *The Four Seasons*

Antonio Vivaldi
(1678-1741)

Spring
From *The Four Seasons*

Antonio Vivaldi
(1678-1741)

Ukulele

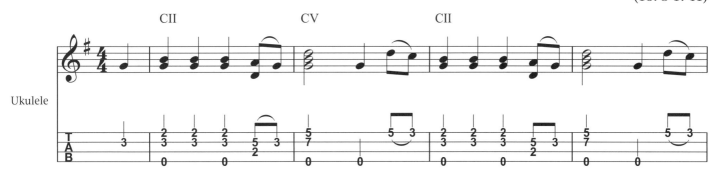

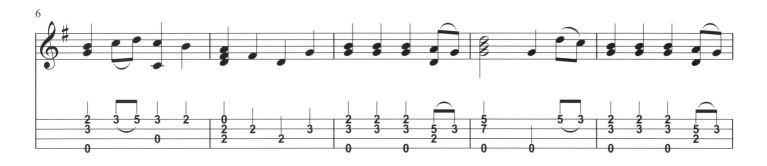

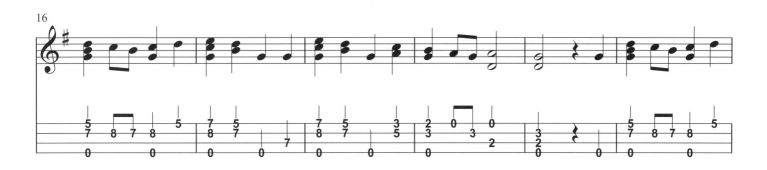

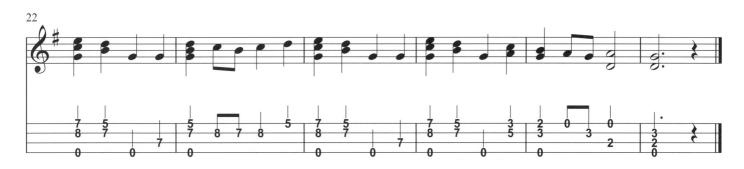

Bourrée
From the *Fourth Cello Suite*

Johann Sebastian Bach
(1685-1750)

Ukulele

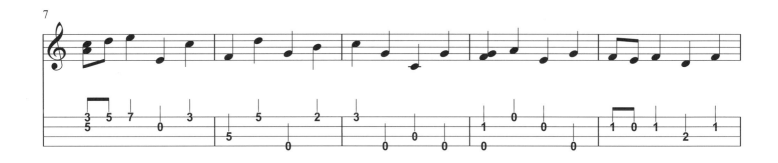

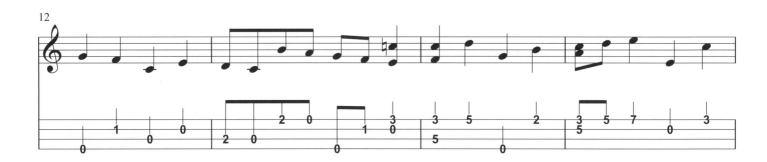

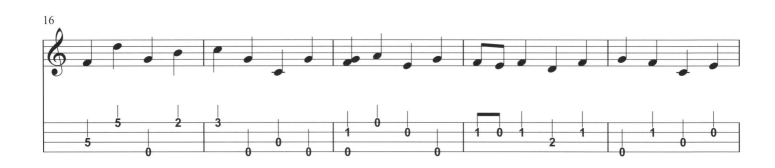

The Harmonious Blacksmith

From *Air and Variations Suite No. 5 in E Major*

George Frideric Handel
(1685-1759)

Rondeau

From *Symphonies de Fanfares*

Jean-Joseph Mouret
(1682-1738)

TRACK 7

Ukulele

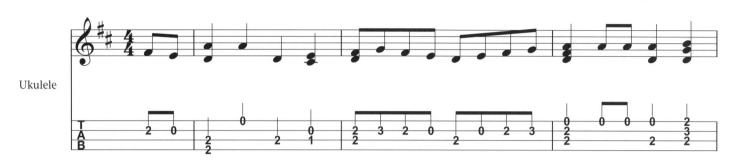

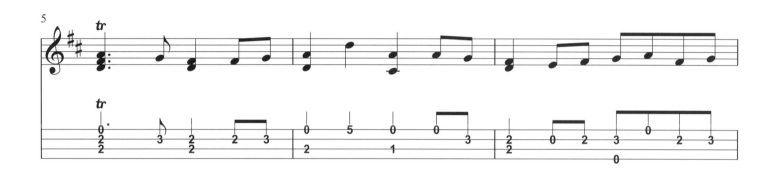

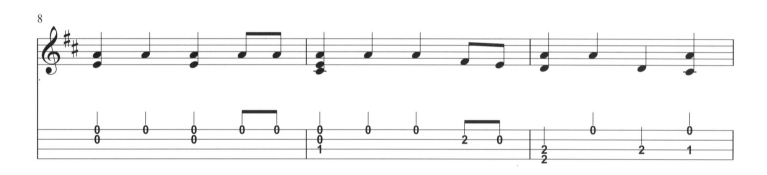

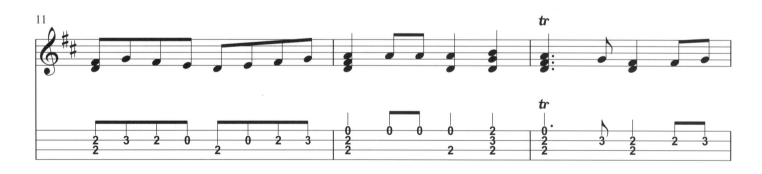

Musette
From *The Anna Magdalena Bach Notebooks*

Johann Sebastian Bach
(1685-1750)

Ukulele

Menuet
From *The Anna Magdalena Bach Notebooks*

Johann Sebastian Bach
(1685-1750)

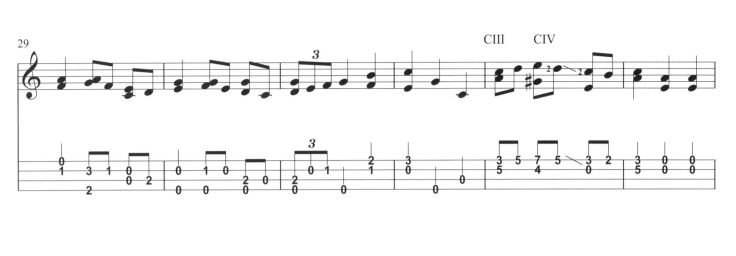

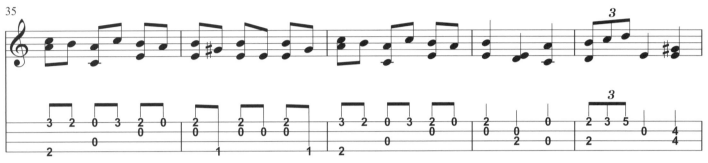

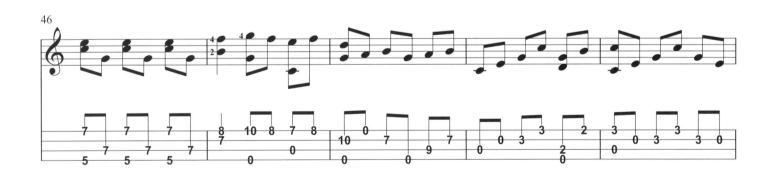

Pièce Pour Luth

Bartlomiej Pekiel
(c. 1610-1670)

Ukulele

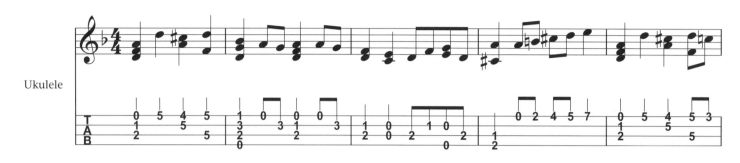

Gavotto

Robert de Visée
(c. 1655-1733)

Ukulele

Minuet II

TRACK 12

Robert de Visée
(c. 1655-1733)

Ukulele

Sarabande

From the *Suite in D Minor*

Robert de Visée
(c. 1655-1733)

Gavotte
From the *Sonata No. 9 in B Flat*

Arcangelo Corelli
(1653-1713)

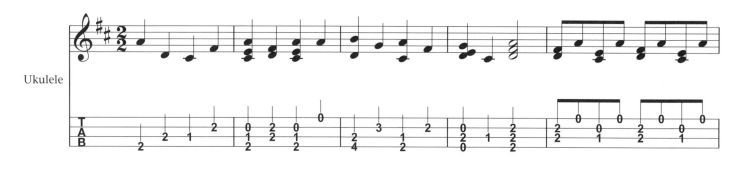

Ukulele

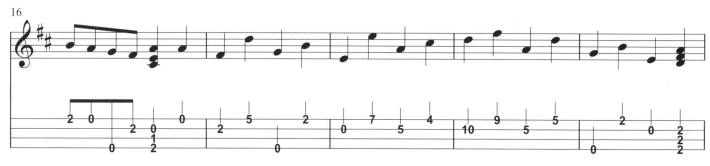

Largo
From *Xerxes*

George Frideric Handel
(1685-1759)

Ukulele

Air On A G String
From *Orchestral Suite No. 3 in D Major*

Johann Sebastian Bach
(1685-1750)

Ukulele

Sleepers Wake

Johann Sebastian Bach
(1685-1750)

TRACK 17

Ukulele

CVIII

10/2015

TRACK 18

Canon

Johann Pachelbel
(1653-1706)

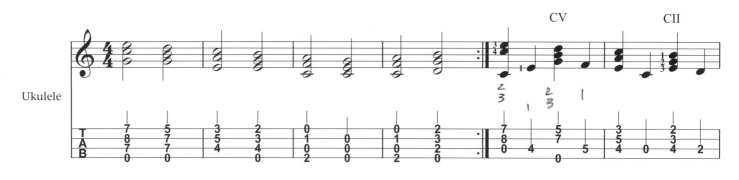

Ukulele

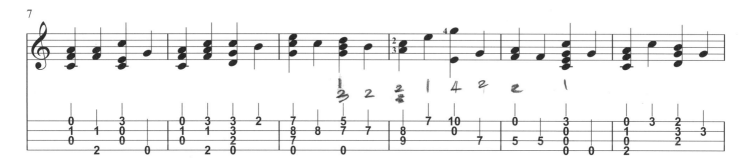

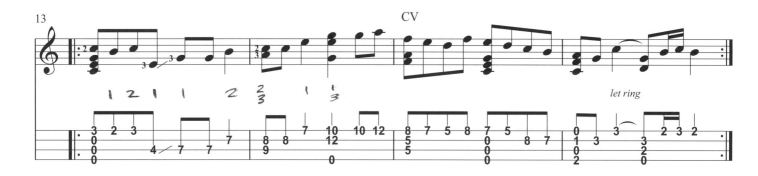

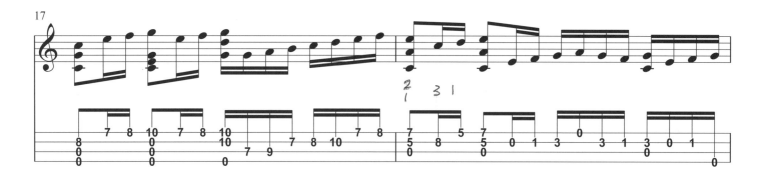

The Prince Of Denmark's March

Jeremiah Clarke
(c. 1674-1707)

TRACK 19

Trumpet Tune

Henry Purcell
(1659-1695)

Bourrée

TRACK 21

Silvius Leopold Weiss
(1687-1750)

TRACK 22

Movement I: Allegro Guisto

From the *Concerto for Lute, 2 Violins and Basso continuo in D Major, RV93*

Antonio Vivaldi
(1678-1741)

Ukulele

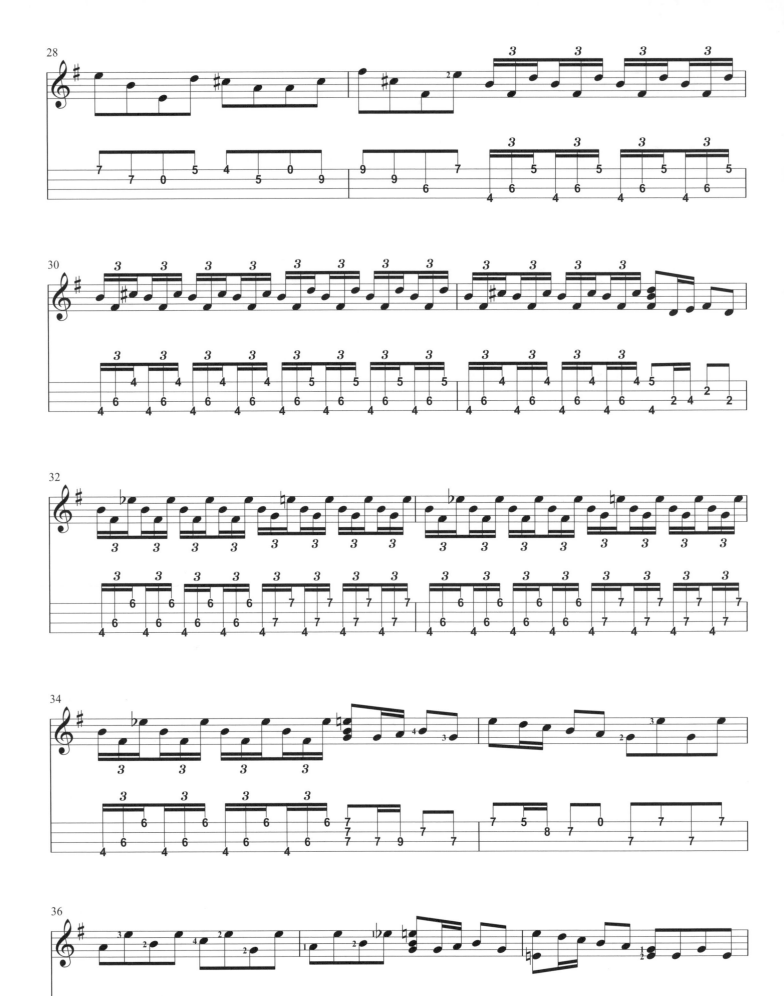

Movement II: Largo

Antonio Vivaldi
(1678-1741)

Ukulele

Movement III: Allegro

Antonio Vivaldi
(1678-1741)

TRACK 24

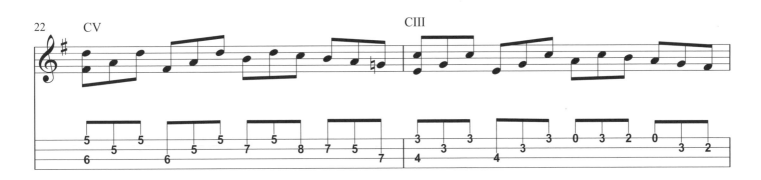

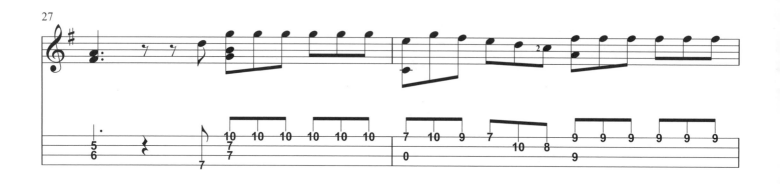

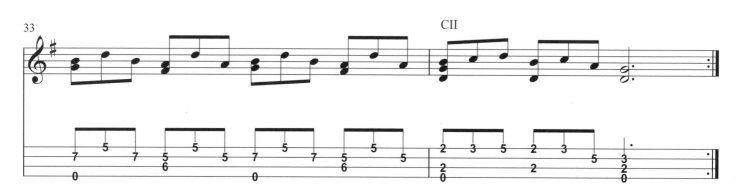